D1708878

COLONIAL FARM

COLONIAL
FARM

by

June Behrens and Pauline Brower

Photographs compiled by Pauline Brower

A Golden Gate Junior Book
Childrens Press • Chicago

To the staff at *Turkey Run* for providing a meaningful experience for the thousands of visitors who have had the opportunity to observe the everyday activities on this early American farm.

ACKNOWLEDGEMENT

The authors wish to acknowledge with thanks the assistance of the *National Park Service* and the following individuals for their contribution to the preparation of the manuscript: Charles A. Veitl, *Superintendent, Turkey Run Park;* David Murphy, *Farm Manager, Turkey Run Farm, McLean, Virginia.*

Our thanks also go to the Turkey Run Farm staff who were photographed as members of the family in the book: Harriet Stout, Spencer Waldron, Jeanne Sheeley, James Ruukles, Libby Sensabaugh and Jay Carney.

We would like to extend our appreciation for their help to: Barbara Dean, *The Colonial Williamsburg Foundation, Williamsburg, Virginia;* Anne Golovin, *Curator, Pre-Industrial Division of Cultural History, Smithsonian Institution;* and to Kurt Fisherkeller, Stephen Ryals and G. R. Sensabaugh for their contribution to the development of the manuscript.

Library of Congress Cataloging in Publication Data

Behrens, June.
　　Colonial farm.
　　"A Golden Gate junior book."
　　SUMMARY: Text and photographs present life on a self-sufficient farm in colonial Virginia.
　　1. Farm life—United States—Juvenile literature. 2. United States—Social life and customs—Colonial period, ca. 1600-1775—Juvenile literature. 3. McLean, Va. Turkey Run Farm—Juvenile literature. [1. Farm life. 2. United States—Social life and customs—Colonial period, ca. 1600-1775. 3. McLean, Va. Turkey Run Farm] I. Brower, Pauline. II. Title.
S519.B45　　975.5'02　　75-28292
ISBN 0-516-08718-5

3 4 5 6 7 8 9 10 11 12 R 80 79 78 77

TURKEY RUN FARM, an 18th century interpretive project of the *National Park Service,* was opened in 1973 so that visitors might see a replica of a working farm at the time our country was struggling to become a new nation. *Turkey Run Farm* is located near the city of McLean, Virginia, off the George Washington Memorial Parkway.

THE COLONIAL AMERICANS lived very different lives from ours today. They made their own clothes. They grew their own food and they built their own homes. They made their living from the land.

On Colonial Farm we see how it was over two centuries ago, just before the American Revolution.

The early American farmer built his house of logs cut from trees in the forest. The logs were set in place, one on top of the other, on the earthen floor. Stone for the fireplace was taken from the fields. Split-log rails were used for fencing orchards and fields. The rail fences kept livestock and wild animals away from the crops.

Let's look in on the Wingfield family who might have lived on Colonial Farm in the colony of Virginia more than two hundred years ago.

Libby Wingfield, along with the rest of the family, woke at sunrise to begin the long work day. Libby slept on a corn-shuck bed in the sleeping loft of the cabin.

Downstairs in the cabin vegetables for the wintertime hung from the rafters. Dried beans, corn, onions, peppers, garlic and herbs would provide the family with

8

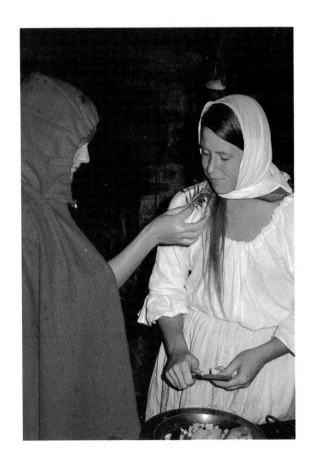

food when the cold weather set in.

Libby's sister Jeanne helped with the morning meal. The Wingfields grew all their own food. They raised pigs and chickens which provided them with meat. Their cows supplied milk. Mother and the girls made butter and cheese from the milk. Mother made a corn bread from dried corn ground into meal.

Wild game from the forest added to the food supply. So did wild tea and other forest plants.

During the summer the Wingfield family dried, smoked and salted some foods to keep them for the winter months ahead. Brother Jay helped Father to net fish in the nearby Potomac River. The fish were first cleaned, then salted down in the fish barrel. In winter Mother went often to the barrel to get food for dinner.

Mother and Libby washed the dishes with lye soap which they had made from hog fat. The dishes were made of clay, wood and a metal called pewter. The large pewter plate was called a trencher. Wooden buckets served as water carriers. Water was heated in an iron kettle over the wood fire.

The woodpile, which was always kept well stocked, provided fuel for cooking and heating the cabin.

Father and Jay planted the crops. But first they had to clear the fields of rocks which they stacked into a neat pile. This was an important part of getting the soil ready.

They often planted corn and beans in the same hill. The corn stalks served as bean poles for the bean vines to grow up on. They planted pumpkins, squash and melons between the hills of corn and beans.

The hoe was an important tool for both Father and Jay. A blacksmith had made the iron hoe head and Father had fashioned the wooden handle from a young tree he had cut down.

Each year Mother, Libby and Jeanne planted a kitchen garden near the house. They planted onions, squash, potatoes, corn and beans in their spring garden. In the fall they planted cabbages and greens.

The girls helped Mother with the sewing. Together they made all the clothes for the family. They carded wool sheared from sheep and Mother spun it into yarn on her spinning wheel. In cold weather the family enjoyed a good supply of warm jackets made from yarn.

Animal skins were used to make shoes and other leather goods. Buttons were handmade, of bone, deer antlers, wood or pewter.

15

Mother and Jeanne dyed the skeins of yarn that hung
from the cabin rafters. Walnut hulls and onion skins in
kettles of hot water colored the yarn brown and yellow.
Red dye was made from insects called cochineal beetles.

Libby helped Mother by bringing in water to cook

with from the water barrel outside. She used a piggin, or dipper, to dip the water from the barrel into a carrying bucket. Sometimes hollow gourds were used as water dippers. The water barrel was filled at a spring not far from the cabin.

Jay helped by carrying in the firewood. He walked on tree bark which had been laid at the doorway to keep mud out of the cabin. The burning wood heated the cabin, cooked the food and provided light in the evening hours.

20

Pumpkin plants grew under the stalks in the corn field. Sometimes Libby, Jay and Father didn't like what they found in the pumpkin patch in the early fall. If there had been a sudden frost the pumpkins wouldn't ripen and the family would not have many to eat during the coming winter. Instead, the green, frost-bitten pumpkins had to be used as feed for the farm animals.

Libby and Jay helped Father to shuck corn. They stripped the outside leaves from the corn ears. The shucks were used for filling the mattresses the family slept on. They made good bedding for the livestock as well.

Both the family and the farm animals ate lots of corn. Father took some of it to the mill where it was ground into corn meal for baking. The miller took part of the meal as payment for grinding the corn.

The hogs on the Wingfield's farm were not penned up until time to fatten them for butchering. They were fed kitchen slop and spoiled food the family couldn't use.

Hogs were an important part of the family diet. Cured hams and bacon kept through the long winter. Fat from the hogs was used for making soap.

The chickens often came right up to the cabin to get their corn. Libby fed them the bad corn the family couldn't eat. She carried it in a handmade linen bag.

The hens laid their eggs just about anywhere on the farm. Jay and Libby had to hunt for them. The chickens provided both meat and eggs for the whole family. Their feathers were sometimes used to stuff mattresses, called "ticks."

Father owned one horse and a few cows. The horse carried many things for him, such as sacks of corn to the mill to be ground.

Father raised cattle mostly for selling or trading for the goods the family needed. The Wingfields did not eat beef very often.

In summer Father usually had a good crop of tobacco. Now and then a neighbor would come by to look at the plants with their healthy wide green leaves.

Like all colonial farmers, Father seldom used money. Instead, he grew tobacco and used it to trade for the things the family couldn't grow or make. Tobacco was called the cash crop. It was traded for salt and sugar, and for hardware such as knives, cooking pots and farm tools.

In the fall the tobacco leaves turned brown. Then they were placed on sticks and hung on the fence to dry. The tobacco was "cured" when the leaves were thoroughly dried. The cured tobacco was then carried to the market in large barrels called hogsheads.

Father taught Jay how to cut the tops off the dried tobacco plants. The seed pods in the tops of the plants would then be stored in the cabin until planting time next spring. The little black seeds in the pods would grow into next year's tobacco crop.

When Mother needed a broom to sweep the earth floor of the cabin Father made it for her. First he made a pole handle, then added long stiff stems of broom-corn. Mother's broom-corn broom helped to keep the cabin clean and comfortable.

Mother taught Libby how to grind dried herbs for medicine. Mother was Libby's teacher. From her Libby learned to cook and sew and to doctor.

Evening was a time for being together after a long and busy day on Colonial Farm.

30

The colonial Americans lived very different lives from ours today. They grew their own food and they built their own homes. They made their living from the land. On Colonial Farm we see how it was two centuries ago, just before the American Revolution...

So begins this unusual book for very young children, picturing in words and graphic illustrations the day-to-day life of a typical colonial farmer and his family as it would have been lived two hundred years ago in the colony of Virginia. We watch as the farmer and his young son clear the rocky land, build the log cabin home, plant the crops and harvest them. We see the wife and two young daughters not only going about the never-ending tasks that kept the family going each day, but spinning and dyeing yarn to make all the family clothing, growing a kitchen garden, preserving meats, fish and vegetables to meet the needs of long winter months ahead. Young readers will enjoy a meaningful experience of "how it was then" through the pages of *Colonial Farm*. The charming photographs were taken "on location" at Turkey Run Farm, an eighteenth-century interpretive project of the National Park Service, near McClean, Virginia.

June Behrens is a reading specialist in one of the largest public school systems in California. A well-known educator, Mrs. Behrens holds a credential in Early Childhood Education and has written more than a score of books for very young readers. She is a graduate of the University of California at Santa Barbara and has a Master's degree from the University of Southern California. Her many books for children reflect her own broad interests, ranging in subject matter from early American history to the metric system. She is the author of three plays to date, published by Childrens Press — *Feast Of Thanksgiving, A New Flag For A New Country* and *The Christmas Magic-Wagon*. She and her husband, a school principal, make their home in Redondo Beach, near Los Angeles.

Pauline Brower has long been interested in American history, particularly the pre-Revolution era. She has traveled extensively throughout the United States exploring the Early American folkways of many regions. Born and educated in Southern California, she now lives in McClean, Virginia, and is an associate editor of the *Northern Virginia Newspapers*, contributing many feature articles on colonial America. She is presently engaged in presenting a Bicentennial lecture series to very young children in Virginia's Fairfax County School District.